PANKAUSKI'S GUARDIANSHIP GUIDE

How your family
will fight over you
& your money

while you are
still alive

JOHN PANKAUSKI

author of
Pankauski's Trustee's Guide:
10 Steps to Family Trustee Excellence
&
Pankauski's Probate Litigation Guide:
Top 10 Probate Mistakes Revealed

authorHOUSE®

AuthorHouse™
1663 Liberty Drive
Bloomington, IN 47403
www.authorhouse.com
Phone: 1 (800) 839-8640

© 2018 John Pankauski. All rights reserved.

No part of this book may be reproduced, stored in a retrieval system, or transmitted by any means without the written permission of the author.

Published by AuthorHouse 10/17/2019

ISBN: 978-1-5462-6865-9 (sc)
ISBN: 978-1-5462-6864-2 (e)

Library of Congress Control Number: 2018913642

Print information available on the last page.

Any people depicted in stock imagery provided by Getty Images are models, and such images are being used for illustrative purposes only.
Certain stock imagery © Getty Images.

This book is printed on acid-free paper.

Because of the dynamic nature of the Internet, any web addresses or links contained in this book may have changed since publication and may no longer be valid. The views expressed in this work are solely those of the author and do not necessarily reflect the views of the publisher, and the publisher hereby disclaims any responsibility for them.

DISCLAIMER

The scenarios in this book involve legal concepts which vary from state to state, case to case, and from time to time. This book contains mere thoughts and perspective, and expressions of opinion only, which may or may not be applicable to issues which you or your family may face.

Guardianship law is absolutely evolving. No single book will guide you through all guardianship matters, but this one is intended to provide you with perspective. *Insight.* Perhaps you will gain information and background which you did not previously have; and this will help you with your estate plan and also planning for your incapacity.

If you are faced with a pending guardianship, or if you are thinking about *"filing one"*, this book will give you a taste for what you are in for. While death and taxes may be certain, is incapacity also just down the road? What does incapacity mean for families? And your money?

No book or stranger can replace the advice and counsel of a caring, experienced guardianship lawyer or estate attorney. Some call these attorneys *"elder law"* lawyers. You should get one. I don't write wills or trusts, and don't prepare powers of attorney, so I am unbiased in suggesting that you hire a good probate lawyer who will be in your corner, planning your estate and guiding you through the years. Pick one who is expected to outlive you and your loved one(s).

CONTENTS

Disclaimer v
Introduction... ix

Chapter 1... 1
Chapter 2... 9
Chapter 3... 17
Chapter 4... 27
Chapter 5... 35
Chapter 6... 45
Chapter 7... 57
Chapter 8... 67

Conclusion... 73
Index 77
About the Author 85

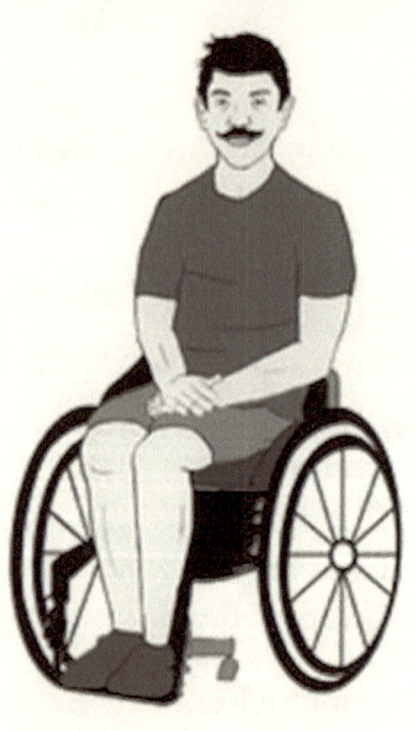

INTRODUCTION

Guardianship litigation is exploding.

The number of guardianship cases relating to adults –<u>not</u> minors or children— filed every year is increasing. That is to say, the number of times which a family member seeks court intervention to determine one's mental capacity is rising.

Guardianship matters, like most lawsuits or civil matters which end up in court, can be simple and easy going, or complex, extensive, and expensive.

We can imagine a "simple" guardianship which is straightforward. A family member with no estate plan needs care, someone to make decisions, and also protection and management of their property.

Indeed, not every guardianship case is "adversarial" or confrontational or "litigious," like we think of most civil lawsuits or court filings.

Many times, a guardian should be appointed by a court to make decisions for a family member or loved one who is not able to make those decisions alone. Or, that family member is simply not capable of making any decisions. Often, someone needs to have a guardian appointed to safeguard and manage one's property. And one's person!

However, let's be truthful: the number of "contested" guardianship cases, is also increasing.

Guardianship wars.

Why do we care? Because we are all living longer, and as longevity increases, mental acuteness decreases. This can, or will, happen to you. It *is* happening to all of us. Right now.

My mom had dementia. I saw it, and its progression, first hand.

Every day, and day to day.

For almost two years.

While it was tough to witness, and quite sad, I did not have guardianship wars to contend with. That, however, is what I, and the litigators and appellate attorneys, deal with every day at our law firm and in our Florida probate litigation practice.

Many you will may have a family member afflicted by mental decline or advanced years. How you deal with that *legally* is a big part of this book.

So....what is meant by *guardianship wars*?

Here's your typical example of a guardianship war: Second and third spouse in their 60s or 70s "fighting" with adult stepchildren who are in their 30s, 40s, and 50s.

Sibling rivalries are played out daily in probate courts, as brothers and sisters vie for control over their parents'—and their parents' money and personal freedoms.

Why has guardianship litigation exploded? There are, primarily, four reasons.

First, Americans are living longer, and we have a greater chance than ever before of being incapacitated before we die. Along the way, we may be in a downward spiral of mental decline making us susceptible to others.

Our life expectancy has increased, and many Americans are living very active, fruitful lives in their 70s and 80s. Take my own parents, for example. My mom had 87 really good years. My dad: 84. Their 70s were active. Their 80s were also just fine. They were alert, oriented, participatory, involved in their grandchildren's lives, interested in traveling to Florida for the winter, and, by all accounts, enjoying a full and fruitful life. That is, until the very last year.

I can remember when I first moved to West Palm Beach, Florida in 1995 – now over 20 years ago. I was in love with the warm weather, the sunshine, the palm trees and the beach. I've always been very active, and I'd taken up jogging when I was in law school. So, when I moved to West Palm Beach, I looked for road races and 5k's to run in. The very first road race that I ran in, in Florida, was in West Palm Beach. And I remember that day vividly.

I recall stretching out before the race and seeing three men, clearly in their 70s, approach the starting point. It was a perfect, sun-filled, warm, pleasant Florida day in November, 1995. They, too, began stretching out, and we started to chat. I was amazed that, here they were, in their 70s, at about 7 AM on a Saturday, ready to compete with many participants who were about a third of their age. There were runners in that race who could have been their grandchildren or great grandchildren.

"The secret" one told me "is to stay active. Get up and get out."

"I've got to ask" I began "................ how old are you?"

"I'm 72. He's 70" pointing to his fellow joggers "he's 76."

"Hats off to you, man" I said. "Honestly, I hope I'm doing this when I'm your age. You guys are an inspiration."

"Get up. And just get out" the silver haired man said, smiling, as if he had a secret, or an edge, or something that I just didn't.

Didn't Edison move to Fort Myers for his health, and didn't he end up living years longer than his doctors expected?

Well, we may never have found the physical, geographic fountain of youth—the destination–in the Sunshine State, but we may have found it in a different sense: staying warm, in the sunny climate, and staying active. Getting up, and, getting out.

Regardless, we're all living longer, more fruitful lives. Than ever before. And as we age, our bodies, knees, hips, may or may not be the first things to go. But they may not be the last. Our bodies are resilient. They can keep going like that Energizer bunny. But our minds, well..................... they can begin to decline, too. But.....

Unlike a sore back, a ground-down knee, or a hip needing a cortisone shot, cartilage injections or replacement, mental decline is not always easy to observe, or feel. It doesn't "bark" pain like a bad knee or arthritis or sore joints. We, and perhaps even some of those around us, may not notice it as quickly as we should. Or, if or when we do notice the mental decline, we don't realize it is as *severe* as it may be. We may not realize the rate of *progression*. Yes, our mental decline, and the *rate* of mental decline, may not be as readily apparent as our physical declines.

Anyway, we have a greater likelihood than any other generation before us of becoming incompetent or incapacitated before we die. As we live longer.

Second, going hand in glove with the first point, advancements in home healthcare, medical services, treatments, and drugs, are all helping us to not only live longer, but also in a diminished, or diminishing, mental state.

Many people now have visiting nurses, nurses aids, or caretakers, which would have been unimaginable a generation before. The cost alone would have been prohibitive. And while, today, the fees for aids and assistants certainly cannot be called "affordable", such services are available on a large scale.

Certain drugs can assist with slowing the progression of dementia. But when we've already lost a certain percentage or amount of our short term memory or analytical abilities, it's gone.

There is one noted neurologist in Palm Beach County who believes that the development and use of two "dementia drugs" are nothing short of "miraculous."

Yes, advances in medicine and science are not only helping us live longer, but can also help us keep our marbles—or, what we have left of them. Of course, the challenge seems to be trying to detect the diminishing of one's mental capacity early on. The noted neurologist who I just mentioned is quick to point out, when he interviewed my mom, that a loss of short-term memory can be complete and irreversible. Once, say, 15% of your short term memory is gone.... it's gone, and you "ain't" getting it back. The best one can hope for is to <u>slow</u> the progression of memory loss, and loss of mental faculties. As our mental abilities and analytical skills decline as we age, we become increasingly reliant on others.

Third, adult children in their 30s-60s seem to be more apt to initiate guardianship litigation, or litigation in general, than any other generation before. Baby boomers, Gen X, Gen Y, and, soon to be, the Millennials, are more apt to seek redress in the courts. I guess that's a polite way of saying everyone after the World War II generation is more likely to sue someone than ever before.

What are they suing over?

You and your money!

I talked about this in my other two books on family money feuds: ***Pankauski's Trustee's Guide*** and ***Pankauski's Probate Litigation***.

In the probate context, such as estate and guardianship matters, or the trust context, today's America is more likely to question a fiduciary's fees, hire an attorney, question how someone is handling money or an inheritance, and to take action — that is, hire a law firm like mine to either initiate or defend family money litigation. What I call the "***fight for blood and money.***" Family members, connected by blood or marriage, fighting over person and purse or property (money.) This includes trying to control mom or dad –and their money, and their estate plan – as they age.

Finally, these post-WWII generations are impatient. In this fast food, microwave-on-high, good-to-go, ready-fire-aim America, no one wants to wait anymore, especially for an inheritance— and even more so when they see it being "squandered." And we can argue over what it means to squander money. Heck, that's what probate litigators and judges do all day, every day, right? In short, adult children want their inheritance now, and woe to the ones who are "blowing it" – including mom or dad or their latest spouse.

Adult children who believe that you are spending **your** money imprudently, or needlessly, want to have a say in **your** financial matters, so they can try to stop it, change it or control it.

Heck, you or your guardian, or trustee, or your latest spouse or power-of-attorney, spending **your money** on **your care**, and nurses aids, health care workers, nurses assistants, car services, all means less of an inheritance for them.

You'll learn shortly that a guardianship court is the venue for that family money fight. Disapproving adult children who live hundreds of miles away from dad get upset when dad lavishes his new girlfriend from Palm Beach with gifts.

Step-parents are pitted against adult step-children.

2nd and 3rd spouses "battle" for their spouse's money against the greedy, un-caring adult children from a prior relationship. And vice versa. Adult children don't want mom or dad's latest spouse to "take" all their inheritance.

That's right. Adult children hate to see their mother's or father's second, third, or fourth spouse spending what these adult children regard as "***their*** inheritance" — their parents' money, their family money.

It used to be that *the old way of doing business* was to fight over money *after* mom and dad both died. Will contests. Probate fights. Trust lawsuits.

Typically, siblings and other heirs at law fought over an inheritance when both mom and dad were gone. Sure, they were divvying up the silverware and family heirlooms, and already spending their expected inheritances, in the limo on the way to the funeral, but it was ***after*** mom or dad died.

With the high rate of divorce, this typically happens when mom **or** dad dies. Adult children battle with the then boyfriend, girlfriend, partner, "friend" or surviving second or third spouse. Yes, they are not only counting their inheritance in the limo on the way to the burial, but a probate litigator is already on speed-dial.

But death is too long to wait to fight over purse and property, isn't it? Mom or dad are living longer. And they are slipping. Their money is at stake and at risk— to **financial predators** or those who financially **exploit the elderly**, or.... other family members.

Whether it's siblings vying to control mom or dad, and their money, or siblings united against mom or dad's latest spouse, people are not waiting for the burial to call their litigator. They are filing guardianship lawsuits, seeking to control their parents' *human rights* and *civil liberties* and their money and property. Right now.

Guardianship wars.

Yes, guardians and guardianships are not for just minors, not just for those under 18 years of age. We are talking about a court action which will determine whether an *adult* has the **mental capacity** to act on their own, and, if not, what rights will, or will not, be removed by a court of law.....and who gets to control the money when a judge says that mom or dad can't.

And let's be clear, please: not all guardianship cases are vicious or antagonistic. Many are filed by caring individuals who recognize that an aging or failing parent needs assistance, protection. Many guardianship cases are sincere and needed. But I'm not going to be talking about those in this book. I'm going to talk about how the guardianship court has become a new battlefield of the probate wars.

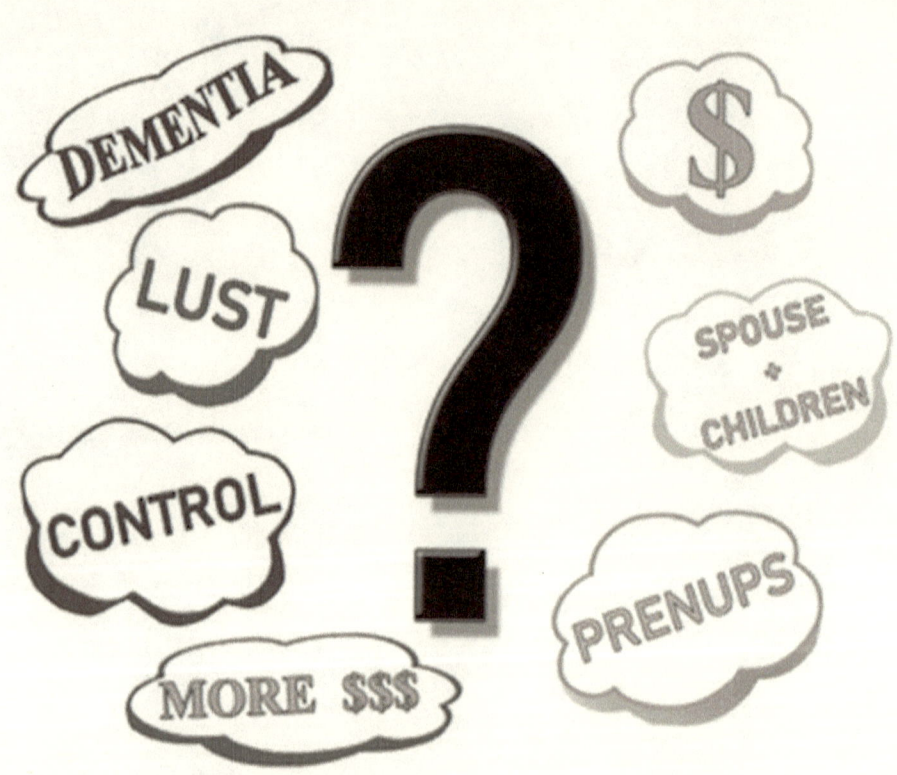

CHAPTER 1

why guardianship?

what is a guardianship lawsuit, or proceeding, or legal action?

In the introduction, we discussed how people are living longer, and are susceptible to mental decline even as their bodies, albeit slower, and sorer, hold out. We also discussed how people are more apt to sue, or file a lawsuit, than ever before—especially where money or control is involved.

And that is what a guardianship is all about: **control.**

Who will control your person, and personal decisions, and your purse (or property)?

A guardianship lawsuit may be well-intentioned, and even necessary. Why?

Because someone who is incapacitated, or who just can't handle their legal or business affairs anymore, needs assistance. They need to be protected. Cared for.

> Guardianship litigation is about control….control over your person, property and purse !

Sometimes, the trial lawyers in my West Palm Beach law firm receive calls from nice family members who, selflessly, need to "open" a guardianship because mom or dad is slipping.

However, there is also a more "stressful",

expensive, and confrontational, or adversarial, side to that "legal coin."

Family members call me when there is trouble. Contention. Disagreement. A legal fight.

Our firm is a litigation firm, after all. We are hired to resolve disputes. Someone maybe started the fight, but we will end it. We don't get hired when everyone gets along and trusts one another. No, the lawyers in my law firm are getting calls each week to **litigate:** when family members <u>don't</u> get along. When one person wants to control mom or dad…..and someone else does not want that person to have the power.

The new **battleground** in the **probate wars** is the guardianship court.

The "*fight for your wealth*", what I call the fight over "blood and money" – how adult children, siblings, and 2nd and 3rd spouses, step-parents and step-children, engage in the "**probate wars**"— is no longer limited to an estate battle <u>after</u> the death of someone.

The guardianship wars go on now, while you are alive, and maybe (maybe not) while you are still competent.

The guardianship court is the venue, the "stadium" or ball park, for the fight for your wealth—while you are still alive and kicking.

In this case, since you are still alive, it's also a fight over your personal, **civil liberties** and

human rights. More on that, and just what a guardianship proceeding is, in Chapter 2.

But first.... A few words about "probating" your estate when you die......

You see, when you die, even if your estate planning attorney promised that you could **avoid probate** with a revocable or *living trust*, there still may be a probate, and a probate war, if someone is **objecting to the will**. There may also be other reasons why a probate is opened. A probate proceeding is more than the mere filing of a will with the county clerk or the clerk of courts.

When we refer to "opening a probate" or "probate", we often mean, or speak to, the creation of a legal action and proceeding, with lawyers, court-filed documents, and a case number—all to administer your estate when you pass. Assets are to be gathered, and accounted for, debts are to be paid, expenses are to be paid, final income tax returns should be prepared and filed, perhaps even a U.S. Federal Estate Tax Return.

Petitions or motions are filed in probate proceedings seeking legal relief, and orders are given out by a judge for all to follow. Property is given, or taken away, authority is granted to **executors** or *personal representatives*, and wealth can be distributed, or shifted.

And estate attorneys are paid.

A lot.

Especially if everyone is fighting.

Just what can go wrong when planning your estate, or administering your probate or estate when you die, is the subject of my second book, which is already published, ***Pankauski's Probate Litigation Guide: Top 10 Probate Mistakes Revealed***.

But what we are talking about in **this** book, ***Pankauski's Guardianship Wars***, is the fight for your wealth ......***right now!***

In most states, the court system, or judicial process, has a court devoted to hearing guardianship matters— typically, the probate court. In Florida, for example, and certainly in Palm Beach County, the probate court hears cases not only about estates, probates and guardianships, but also trusts. You see, the probate division is different than the "family" (divorce) division, or the juvenile division, or the criminal division.

The filing of a guardianship action, then, permits the *legal actors*—adult children, spouses, your trustee, so-called **"interested persons"**— to be heard on whether you've "got it", are "with it", and whether you need some protection and assistance.

Or not. (That's a polite way of saying that your family can, or may, come into court to control you and your money. .....The fight over power and purse.)

Are you an adult child who thinks that dad has lost his marbles and is now doing crazy things with his money (and his 2nd wife or new girlfriend)?

Are you a loving daughter who is concerned that your mother may be financially exploited by that new tennis pro or bridge partner to whom mom has written significant checks?

Perhaps you are the successor trustee of dad's revocable trust, and you learned that his doctor does not believe he can manage his financial affairs?

Well, the guardianship court is the venue or place to step in and be heard. And as long as you have some connection to the person who you are "filing guardianship" over, this is the chance to say your peace.

You see, relatives are not the only ones who can file a guardianship action, or participate in a guardianship proceeding. While it's true that strangers can't necessarily come in and be involved in a guardianship case, **interested persons** can.

What's an **interested person**?

Although it can depends on the facts and circumstances of each case, an interested person is almost always your spouse and children, maybe your grandchildren, and perhaps your siblings, parents, other relatives, ex-spouses, doctors, lawyers, the successor trustee of your revocable trust, your caretakers and even your neighbor.

Of course, one can also demonstrate that blood relatives, like children, are <u>not</u> concerned about your welfare, are <u>not</u> involved in your life, and should not participate in the guardianship proceeding: they are not an *interested person*.

So, if someone with a connection to you believes that you may need some assistance, some oversight, maybe even some protection, or that your money and property is at risk, or may need to be managed, then the guardianship court can be the venue to ask the court to intervene in your personal and financial life. If you are unable to manage your affairs, a guardianship may be proper.

Maybe.

Maybe not.

But be ready!

Because the filing of a guardianship case is not always done to protect someone who needs some assistance. It can also be filed to fight over your money, and who will control you.

CHAPTER 2

what is a guardianship?

understanding the process now, can assist you, and your loved ones, later

In Chapter 1, we learned that a guardianship court case can be the "venue" to try to control you and your property while you are still alive and kicking.

It may be based upon good, sincere and helpful motives: you are in mental decline and need assistance, so someone close to you "filed for guardianship" to help you.

But guardianship cases can also be the **battleground** where those close to you fight over blood and money: a new battle ground in the *probate wars*.

A guardianship case involves somebody, often called the **"*petitioner*"**, who files a guardianship petition, asking important questions, or making a very strong suggestion: does somebody need to have some, or all, of his or her rights removed by the guardianship court because they are partially or totally ***incapacitated***?

This may come as a surprise, indeed, even a shock, to many: the truth is that a probate court judge in a guardianship proceeding is going to determine whether a person, called the ***alleged incapacitated person***, or AIP, is *competent* or not competent, and to what degree.

Throughout this legal process, the guardianship court will determine whether the *alleged incapacitated person* is capable of exercising some, or all, of his or her own rights.

If the guardianship court believes that the *alleged incapacitated person* is not able to exercise some, or all, of his or her rights, the guardianship court will make a finding on what rights should be **taken away** from the *AIP* and who should exercise those rights.

As you'll see in the following two chapters, a **guardian** may or may not be appointed. Much of that will depend on whether a **lesser restrictive alternative** to a "full blown," court-supervised, round-the-clock guardianship can *adequately* address the needs of the *alleged incapacitated person*.

Put another way: a guardianship court will determine whether you need a "partial" guardianship or a total or "**plenary**" guardianship, and, if so, what rights should be taken away from you and who will be given authority over you and/or your property.

If you can manage your affairs, just fine, and are competent, then you don't need a guardianship. If however, you are NOT capable of handling some or all of your affairs, whether due to mental or physical decline, advanced years, dementia or otherwise, then a guardian may be appointed to help you with some or all of your personal and financial matters.

In some instances, an **emergency** *temporary guardian* may be appointed if there are allegations of irreparable harm or danger which may result if immediate action is not taken. Ask any probate litigator and they will tell you that some lawyers abuse this process. They file "emergency" guardianship petitions when no real emergency exists.

The guardianship court may have a guardianship that is very limited, and narrow in scope, or one that is very broad in scope, over you, your "person" (which involves your **civil liberties** and **human rights**) and, perhaps, your property.

In every guardianship case that my West Palm Beach law firm has been involved in, we always try to figure out the "back story." Hell, we need to know it, because the judge in the probate court is looking for the same thing. And he or she is going to try to figure out what's really going on here pretty quickly.

Who's the "good guy" and who's the "bad guy?"

Who is the "loving daughter" or "evil daughter"?

Why was a guardianship filed? Is there a sincere motive to assist someone who truly needs help, or is there another motive? Family money fueds? Sibling rivalry? After all, guardianship cases are serious business.

So, what is a guardianship, and what happens when a guardianship case is filed?

Well, first and foremost, as hinted at previously in the book, we are not talking about a guardian for a minor, someone under

18. Guardians may be appointed for a minor when a parent is not there. And even when a parent is there, a *guardian ad litem* may be appointed by the court to look out for and protect a minor's interests. This is common in many trust lawsuits or settlements.

In this book, however, we are talking about an **adult person** who may need some assistance—so much so, that a court is involved and that court may, or may not, appoint a guardian to be in charge of some, or all, of your life and your money.

A guardianship court, then, is a specially designed venue, just like "family law" divisions of courts which handle divorces, alimony issues and child custody and support. The criminal division deals with the state charging people with crimes. The civil division handles trials like breach of contract, negligence. The foreclosure division....well, you've got it.

Guardianships cases for adults have been increasing so much that many states not only have a special court for guardianship practice, but its own set of rules and laws. In Florida, we have certain "probate rules" which can apply. Chapter 744 of the Florida Statutes is referred to as the **Guardianship Code** and deals exclusively with laws for guardianships.

While we can argue whether guardianship cases are filed for the wrong reasons or not, the truth is that a guardianship practice is now a common component to a probate litigation law firm's practice, just like estate disputes, will contests, surviving spouse rights and actions to replace a trustee.

If you asked me 20 years ago if I was going to handle guardianship cases, my answer would have been a quick and short "no." Now, our law firm is discussing guardianship matters, or in guardianship court, each and every week of the year.

Guardianship litigation is an important part of our firm's practice, and, no doubt, an important part of many "**elder law**" lawyers' practices. But unlike so called "elder law" lawyers, or estate planning or probate lawyers, our firm does not "write" or "draft" wills, trusts and estate plans. We only litigate.

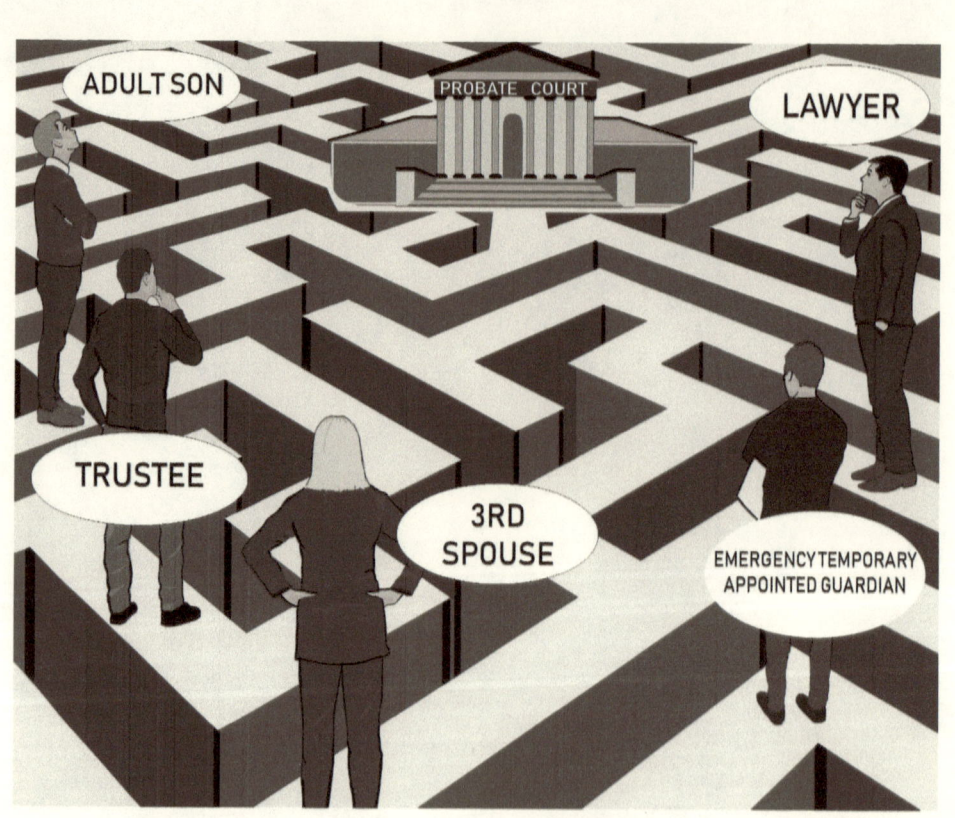

CHAPTER 3

getting through the guardianship maze

What does a guardianship case look like?

There are five things that you need to know about a court filed guardianship. I'm going to summarize these five characteristics or criteria in a very broad, general way. My hope is that you will obtain an understanding of the guardianship court's role in an adult guardianship proceeding, and what happens when someone "files for guardianship."

A guardianship is "opened," or "filed," by the filing of a **petition** or "complaint" with a court of law. The petition or complaint will make allegations that someone needs some assistance because they are not capable of exercising all or some of their rights. The matter will be assigned to a judge or a division within the court system. If there is a request for an emergency guardian, the court will be given the file right away by the clerk's office; and the court may appoint an **emergency temporary guardian** who can be given authority right away. All with the stroke of a pen. The judge's pen.

If a guardianship has been filed against you, here's what will happen. The guardianship court will 1) appoint an attorney to represent you; 2) appoint an ***examining committee*** to meet with you, interview you, and file a report; 3) hold a hearing, or a trial, to determine whether you are partially or completely **incapacitated**; and 4) determine whether a guardianship is appropriate, and if so; 5) determine who the guardian or guardians should be.

When a guardianship case is filed, there may actually be two cases: a **"mental health"** case and a *"guardianship"* case. The role of the guardianship court will be to **determine your mental capacity** and determine whether you are *competent* or not competent, whether you **lack capacity** or have all, or some, of your faculties.

Put another way, a probate court will determine whether you are partially or totally incapacitated, or whether you have capacity, in which case, a guardianship would not be needed.

Wait a minute!

A judge is going to determine *mental* capacity?

A non-doctor?

A judge.......who does not have a medical degree?

Yes, that's right.

A judge will weigh the evidence before him or her, and make a decision. Even if it's a tough call. That's what our judges do....every day. But it's OK.

I can tell you first hand from having appeared in so many guardianship cases, that in the probate court, that is, the "guardianship court", judges take guardianship cases very, very seriously. That's a really good thing.

Judges know that they are dealing with a human life, civil liberties and rights. They understand this. The probate courts bend over backwards to look out for the **alleged incapacitated person**, to give him or her the opportunity to be heard, and, if there is a concern of possible exploitation, to protect that individual.

Guardianships can turn a life upside down. They are invasive and, sometimes, even questionable. Imagine that you get a knock on the door and it's a lawyer you have never met, explaining that he or she has been appointed by a court to represent you.

Who?

What?

Then the phone starts ringing off the hook: psychologists or maybe a doctor, perhaps a health care professional, or one without a medical degree, telling you that they are coming over to interview you. Examine you. They explain that they are members of the **examining committee** appointed by a judge to, well, judge you.

What?

Guardianships can pit family members against each other. Courts know this. And that's a good reason to find the *back story*, and learn if anyone is the "bad guy" or "bad girl."

The guardianship court typically appoints an **examining committee** to conduct an examination of the alleged incapacitated person. Members of the examining committee are typically people who are involved in healthcare, elder matters, or medicine. The state does not pay examining committee members a lot of money. Not all examining committee members may be doctors, let alone doctors with a psychiatric, neurological or mental health background. Each examining committee member will meet with the alleged incapacitated person personally, and prepare a written report which will be submitted to the court.

This **written report** will reveal opinions, observations, and will make specific recommendations, including whether one has capacity or not, whether a total or ***plenary guardianship*** is needed, or whether only a *partial* guardianship is needed. Additionally, the examining committee reports will suggest what *rights should be removed* from, or taken away from, the alleged incapacitated person.

As you might imagine, the examining committee reports are often criticized and the subject of legal wrangling. These reports can be **evidence**—very strong evidence— in a guardianship trial, although they are "hearsay" documents which may necessitate the live testimony of each examining committee member at a hearing or guardianship trial.

The probate court will also appoint an attorney, counsel, to represent the alleged incapacitated person in this proceeding. Many times, the alleged incapacitated person already has a long time,

21

long-standing attorney who may or may not replace the court appointed counsel. But courts want a lawyer looking out for, and fighting for, the alleged incapacitated person. The alleged incapacitated person gets someone –the court appointed counsel — who only answers to the person "accused" (alleged) to be incapacitated.

Guardianship courts typically give great credence to, and pay close attention to, all the thoughts and recommendations of the alleged incapacitated person's **attorney**, and the examining committee members. A sister may be fighting to control mom, while another child of mom's doesn't want sister to get control. Or a son may be attempting to be appointed the guardian of father, against the wishes of father's 2nd spouse.

Lawyers for those family members, or *legal actors,* are all advocates: advocating for their own clients, and not necessarily the best interests of the alleged incapacitated person.

But the court appointed counsel, the attorney for the alleged incapacitated person, well, he or she has no agenda other than to look out for and protect his or her client: the person who is the subject of the guardianship proceedings.

The alleged incapacitated person generally does not need to testify or even be heard in his or her own guardianship case. His or her lawyer, however, will take steps to be heard, and advocate on behalf of the alleged incapacitated person. Of course, family members and other **interested persons** involved in the guardianship ......they make their case.

And talking about making a case..... the probate judge will set the matter for a "hearing". But don't be fooled. This is actually a **guardianship trial**. With rules of evidence and burdens of proof. Don't let the word "hearing" fool you. When the court sets a date and time to determine whether one is incapacitated or not, this is a big deal. The same goes for a hearing on who should be the guardian. Serious stuff. Trial work.

I run into a lot of lawyers who call themselves "probate" or "guardianship" or "elder law" attorneys. These lawyers claim to handle a lot of guardianship matters. But they don't know the first thing about evidence, the rules of courtroom procedure, how to get documents admitted, how to cross examine or impeach a witness, or how to try to keep evidence out. While it is very important to know about guardianship law, when there is a trial, you need someone with, well, trial skills. Many elder law lawyers just don't litigate or conduct trials, even though they may go to court a lot.

So, you will have your day in court, and the judge will determine if you are in need of a guardian, and, if so, who the guardian(s) will be.

There may be a guardian of your *person* and/or your property. There may be one guardian who handles all that important "stuff", or, there may be two: one guardian to make personal decisions for you (a guardian of *your person*) and one guardian to handle your money (a guardian of your *property*). Unless, of course, there is an alternative....................

CHAPTER 4

alternatives to guardianship

You may be able to avoid a guardianship, or the appointment of a guardian, if there is a **lesser restrictive alternative** to a court-supervised, "full blown" guardianship that *adequately* addresses your needs.

Boy, that sounds like lawyer-speak, doesn't it?

<u>Consider this</u>: Is there a way to avoid a guardianship if you plan carefully, now, while you are competent?

With your estate planning lawyer?

Indeed, there is.

When you plan your estate, talk to your estate planning attorney about **planning for incapacity**. If you do it correctly, you can do an "end run" around a guardianship proceeding, if one is filed someday in the future.

Even if you are in need of assistance, that is to say, even if you are partially incapacitated, you may not need a guardian. Or, to put it another way, a guardianship court may not need to appoint a guardian—even when it's clear that you need one.

Likewise, let's say that the court determines that you are *totally* incapacitated, and you <u>absolutely</u> need assistance and protection, you still may not need a guardian.

A guardian may not be needed if there is a **lesser restrictive alternative** to a court-supervised guardianship that *adequately* addresses your needs. What needs?

> *Even if you need a guardian, you may be able to avoid a guardianship with the proper estate plan.*

A guardianship court is going to consider your own, unique, personal situation—at the time that somebody files a guardianship petition concerning you. This includes where you may be living, how you are living, how your daily needs are being attended to, and how your property or money is being safeguarded. Oh yes, the guardianship court should also consider **your intent**.

But wait, how can a person who is partially or totally incapacitated have their intent conveyed to the guardianship court?

Your intent can be apparent from your existing estate plan. That is to say, you can plan your legal, personal, and financial affairs, now, while you are competent.

Plan for what?

Plan for death: certainly. That's what most people think of when they create an estate plan. But....also plan for the day that you may be incapacitated. And unable to make decisions.

Yes, estate plans are not just for dying anymore. Increasingly, estate lawyers and probate attorneys are speaking to clients about who they want in charge if they lose capacity.

Most courts have a legal process which recognizes that even if you may be declining, a guardianship may not be necessary or appropriate if you have already set in motion a process, or a mechanism, to adequately address your needs when you are unable to help yourself.

Put another way: as part of this process or mechanism, do you have your "team" in place – right now!— to take care of you if you are unable to take care of yourself (in the future)?

What does your estate plan say about incapacity? Who have you selected to make health care decisions for you if you are not able to? Who will be in charge of your property if you can't manage it or handle money? Who will pay your bills, income taxes, real estate taxes, mortgage, rent, and living expenses?

Don't <u>you</u> want to make those decisions of who will help you, perhaps, in the future, right now?

Don't you want to select your "team" now, while you are competent?

If you don't select your advisors and "team" now, and you are later the subject of a guardianship, a judge is going to make those decisions.

So, ask yourself or your estate planning lawyer: is there a process or mechanism in place that will pay your bills, insure that you receive medical attention, are clothed, fed and cared for properly if you can't handle your own affairs? Will your taxes be paid? Will you be comfortable, safe and protected?

There is such a process or mechanism, and estate planning attorneys should be talking to clients about this every day! Indeed, they are writing or drafting **estate plans** which anticipate that you may lose your mental faculties one day; that you may one day become incapacitated and unable to manage your affairs. More so, you can have an estate plan which anticipates that someday, someone may file for guardianship! Indeed.

Why is this important? Because most guardianship courts recognize your right, or your ability, to **predetermine** who will be in charge of all your personal rights, health care decisions, and all your properties and money, if you are unable to care for yourself.

Why, the analysis goes, should a judge, who probably doesn't know you, determine your care, and select your caretakers, if you have already done so according to a valid estate plan? (At a time when you were competent and free from undue influence.)

Said a slightly different way: most guardianship courts will respect the decisions which you made regarding who will exercise your rights and take care of you if, otherwise, a guardianship were needed.

Most guardianship courts will recognize, and give effect to, your choices, or your process or your mechanism to care for you, without the need of a guardian if your estate plan adequately addresses or provides for your needs.

Could your spouse or your adult children, or other people for that matter, attempt to disrupt your choices and your process or mechanism?

Yes, they could.

In fact, they do that by hiring guardianship litigators.

They can argue that your estate plan should not be recognized, or given effect. Family members could argue that the guardianship court should ignore your estate plan.

Guardianship litigation lawyers often argue about whether a guardianship is needed, or not, or whether a lesser restrictive alternative exists.

<u>And even when</u> a lesser restrictive alternative to a guardianship exists, guardianship lawyers, and the court, grapple with whether that alternative is in your **best interests**. Is it *adequate* to protect you? Does it *adequately address your needs*?

Are you ready? Is everything in place? What do you need to know about an alternative to a guardianship?

Well, first of all, most people seem to agree that they would rather not have a court intervene in their lives. After all, an official guardianship is subject to court supervision. Annual reports need to be filed, accountings completed. Oh yes, I almost forgot……. Do you know who pays for all of this?

You do!

But, you say, what if you are incapacitated and don't have the legal ability to pay your bills? Not to worry, the guardian who was appointed to manage all your money and property can cut the check. From your funds, of course.

So, how do you **avoid** a guardianship *in the future*, by putting a plan in place now?

What is this process or mechanism which was hinted at in this chapter to "plan around" or anticipate a possible guardianship?

What in the world is a **lesser restrictive alternative**?

That topic is the subject of chapter 5.

LESSER RESTRICTIVE ALTERNATIVE		**POA**
ADVANCED HEALTHCARE DIRECTIVE	*THIS COURT FINDS YOU NEED A GUARDIAN*	**TRUSTEE**
HEALTHCARE PROXY		**LIVING TRUST**

CHAPTER 5

lesser restrictive alternatives to a guardianship

*when will a court not appoint a guardian,
even when you need one?*

So, **what** is a *lesser restrictive alternative* to a guardianship?

And, **how** can a lesser restrictive alternative adequately address the needs of the person who is the subject matter of the guardianship?

The most common forms of a lesser restrictive alternative include an estate plan that already contemplates incapacity or potential guardianship.

Remember: an estate plan is not simply a will. It can contain other documents which work closely with your will.

Do you have a ***power of attorney***, giving someone authority to assist you with your business or financial affairs like paying your income taxes, or your real estate taxes, or your bills?

What about the management and safeguarding of your property and money?

Most people have a ***revocable*** or ***living trust*** which can adequately safeguard and protect your property. Most revocable or living trusts have you, the creator or, *grantor*, or *settlor*, serve as your first, or initial, trustee.

But what if you become unable to serve as trustee? What if you become incapacitated or cannot adequately handle your business or financial affairs? Well, then you need a successor trustee.

Your revocable trust can spell out who your successor trustee will be if you are unable to serve as your own trustee. This person, **your** chosen successor trustee, can manage your property and money while you are incapacitated. In an earlier chapter, we discussed how a guardianship court may appoint a guardian *of the person* and or a guardian *of the property*.

You don't need a guardian of your property if you have a revocable trust. Why? Because you already have someone to manage and protect your property: your successor trustee. Your successor trustee can pay your bills, pay for your care, pay your income taxes, medical bills, and work with your family members or your other fiduciaries (like your guardian, your attorney in fact, or your health care surrogate or proxy.)

Have you funded your revocable trust? If you have not already transferred your assets to your revocable trust, don't worry. Your **attorney in fact** under your power of attorney can retitle assets in the name of your revocable trust, so your chosen successor trustee is in control. Your *attorney in fact* (power of attorney) can transfer assets which are in your individual name, and not titled in your trust, to your revocable trust, so your trustee can manage your property for you.

Is there real estate out there in your sole name? Are bank accounts in your own individual name? Maybe you have a brokerage account with lots of stocks and bonds. All of those should be safeguarded and protected if you cannot attend to them. If you don't have an attorney in fact to act for you, because, perhaps, you never created a power of attorney, not to worry. The guardianship court can appoint a temporary, or a limited, guardian of your property to fund your revocable trust. This temporary guardian of your property can marshal, or find and retrieve, your assets, and "put them" in your revocable trust.

If this sounds like a lot of legal work, please think again. It's not. We do this all the time.

Here is <u>one important point</u> about powers of attorney: talk to your estate planning lawyer about considering the pro's and con's of a **durable** power of attorney. Why?

A power of attorney is a grant of authority to someone. It's often referred to as an "agency", although the one to whom you give power, or authority to act for you, is often a *fiduciary* under the law. Typically, such an arrangement ends if you become incapacitated. However, the important exception to this rule is a **durable** *power of attorney*: which continues even if you are incapacitated. In fact, an important purpose of creating (signing) a durable power of attorney is specifically so that this document, this relationship, or granting of power, does indeed "survive" incapacity.

Why do you need a full time, or "full blown", guardian of your property if you already have a trust in place? You don't.

In truth, your revocable trust can be your process or mechanism to safeguard and protect your property. Talk to your estate planning attorney about creating a revocable trust. And choose your successor trustees wisely.

Beyond the management of your property and money, what about your **personal rights**, decisions, **human rights** and **civil liberties**?

Who will determine where your residence will be? Who will decide who you can associate with, or visit with?

What about your **medical decisions** and **health care** decisions? Who is going to make the call on what doctors you see? How much of your money is spent on your healthcare, nurses, doctors and nurses assistants? What facility or hospital you reside in or are receiving care at? Who will decide what treatment you will receive? Don't you need a guardian for those important decisions?

Well, with the right power of attorney, and health care documents as part of your estate plan, you may be able to set everything up so that your fiduciaries take care of you if can't take care of yourself. Without a guardian or court supervision.

If you have a durable power of attorney, remember that your "power of attorney" is a fiduciary: what we call an *"attorney in fact."* Your attorney in fact is supposed to act in your best interests. My suggestion is that you have one, and only one, person to act as your attorney in fact. Some clients like to name <u>all</u> their children, or their spouse <u>and</u> their child or children, to serve as their attorneys in fact. Our law firm has found this to be a mistake in most cases. Having a power of attorney *by committee* can be cumbersome, time-consuming and can serve to slow things down. Attorneys in fact can also fight over your care and disagree on things. Consider naming only one person to be your attorney in fact.

But just like the selection of your successor trustees, the selection of who will be your attorney in fact is an important decision. As I wrote in Chapter 6 of my second book, **Pankauski's Probate Litigation Guide: Top 10 Probate Mistakes Revealed**, a power of attorney can be the most "dangerous" document in the world.

Our probate litigation law firm has been involved in a number of matters where an attorney in fact mis-used the power of attorney for their own self-dealing. Such breaches of fiduciary duty are what probate litigators call "conversion" or "civil theft."

Finally, consider detailed **health care documents** which you may want as part of your lesser restrictive alternative. You should consider having healthcare documents in which you appoint someone to make your medical and healthcare decisions for you if you are not able to.

These healthcare documents may include a **living will** which makes known your intent to be sustained, or not sustained, artificially. The most common examples of this are whether you want to be kept alive on a ventilator, or not, or be kept alive by a machine if you are in a **persistent vegetative state**.

A **healthcare proxy**, or a medical or healthcare durable power of attorney, permits you to grant authority to someone to make important health care and medical decisions for you. That person, sometimes referred to heath care agent, or surrogate, or proxy, can make all healthcare decisions for you. And, no, such authority is not necessarily limited to whether or not to end life support. Important medical and healthcare decisions include what drugs to take or alter, what type of treatment you should receive, or not receive, the level of care you can receive and where you should reside. Your health care agent may also be empowered to make more difficult decisions such as authorizing "do not resuscitate" orders and decisions or orders to terminate life support if you cannot live unaided by a machine or medical technology.

Finally, you can sign or execute guardianship documents, where, if it is determined that a guardianship is necessary, you predetermine who you would like your guardian to be.

One final note on a lesser restrictive alternative to guardianship. You should review and re-review your estate plan on a regular basis, perhaps annually. Many people do it after the new year. Some review their important documents each year after tax time.

Regardless, you'll probably forget who you have selected as your decision-makers and fiduciaries. Don't forget that circumstances change over time. Perhaps you chose a loved one years ago to make your decisions, but now, years later, they moved away. Yes, geography, and convenience, matter. Or, your relationship has deteriorated with a son or daughter you had named as your POA or successor trustee. Did you have a "backup"? Did you name successors in your estate planning documents? Do you need entirely new documents?

When you got married again, years ago, for the 2nd or 3rd time, you perhaps did not include your second or third spouse in your estate planning documents. That's not uncommon. But now, years later, a "miraculous" thing happened.

Your last marriage worked out!

Your marriage is actually strong and you both love and trust each other immensely. You care for each other. And you want your last spouse making the calls when it comes to your healthcare, medical decisions, and perhaps even money and property. Have "backups" or successors. Times change. So do circumstances.....and people.

3rd SPOUSE   **LAWYER**   **GUARDIAN**   **ADULT CHILDREN**

CHAPTER 6

guardianship ghosts

5 things you'll never think about (and what your estate lawyer won't warn you of)

Let me share with you five observations in the guardianship wars which the attorneys at my litigation law firm have noticed over the years.

These issues keep rearing their ugly heads. They are what I call the "guardianship ghosts." Apparitions which are not always clear, but sometimes present. Perhaps a bit scary. Maybe things that can keep a client up at night.

1. **The "take nothing" prenup.**

A good prenuptial agreement is great for a bad marriage. But take a look at the other side of that legal coin.

A bad premarital agreement can be awful for a good marriage.

Many of you have been married more than once. And most of you have signed a prenuptial agreement which limits what your latest spouse might receive upon your death, or a divorce. Got it. Makes sense.

Prenups are often very, very important to <u>adult children</u> of a mother or father who has a few dollars, and who may be remarrying. The adult kids want mom or dad to sign a prenup with the new spouse, hoping that their inheritance will not be diminished if the marriage fails, or when mom or dad pass away. I get it. Asset preservation. Asset protection. Keep money in the family, and away from creditors, including possible former spouses. I understand that. I particularly understand keeping family money away from second or third or fourth spouses when a short duration marriage fails — and there is no love there, let alone a relationship.

So, typically, you see many prenups written up as *"I'll keep mine, you keep yours. And if I die or if we divorce, you get nothing."* If the parties divorce or die, then the other party, or the survivor, doesn't get a dime. Each spouse (or former spouse) takes their own, separate property, and goes their own ways. No harm, no foul.

You know, that's not bad if you're viewing marriage from a particular standpoint: a business standpoint. Or a standpoint that you wish to leave absolutely everything to somebody, or something, other than your latest spouse such as your alma mater, your adult children, or grandchildren.

Prenups are a valid, indeed often prudent, document to sign before getting married. Prenups are a rational, cautionary step before knowing whether the marriage will work out or even last. In Florida, prenuptial agreements are common, and repeatedly upheld by courts when prepared properly. Prenups are an important part of your estate plan.

Check.

Got it !

But ......<u>what happens if that second or third marriage with the prenup *works*</u>? And the marriage *lasts*? And there is actually a lot of *love*? And the *intent* of the spouse with all the money *changes*? In other words, what if the spouse with the money wants to indeed leave an inheritance to their spouse who signed the prenup? Shouldn't the prenup be changed to reflect this? Or shouldn't the spouse with the money change his or her will or trust to leave their spouse *something*?

What if there is a desire to leave to your spouse, upon your death, a decent inheritance, rather than nothing (per the prenup?) What if the spouse with the money wants to insure that his or her surviving spouse is well taken care of, because the marriage worked!? Well, it's simple enough, right?

Rip up the prenup! Or, rather, amend it, and give your spouse an inheritance, right? Or, change your will, create a trust, or purchase a life insurance policy with your spouse as the beneficiary.

But....that rarely happens. Especially if the rich spouse starts to decline mentally and starts losing competency. We all know that you can't sign a contract or create a will if you are not competent. And we know that as we decline, and the doctors' appointments, fatigue and discomfort may increase, it's more challenging to alter your estate plan.

So, what happens to that 2nd, 3rd, or 4th spouse who signed the prenup? Well, he or she becomes the caretaker: a loving, doting spouse, who is wiping the chin of the other spouse, who is now, years after the marriage, losing mental capacity. The 2nd or 3rd or 4th spouse gets screwed. Oh yes, and there are large legal bills along the way. And the legal bills get larger when the adult children file for guardianship to have dad or mom declared incompetent. And now the spouse has to ask the guardian, or the trustee, for an allowance to live off of. And, guess what: many times that guardian or trustee is the adult child of the declining spouse with the money.

Guardianship wars.

Can you avoid this scenario or try to plan around it? Indeed.

2. **<u>Your kids hate your spouse.</u>**

While we're on the subject of second or third marriages, let me revisit a theme which I discussed in Chapter 2—*Enemy of the Estate* of **Pankauski's Probate Litigation Guide.**

Adult children hate their parents' second and third spouses. Hell, many times the second or third spouse hates the adult children just as much. And they will fight and fight and fight over one's property and the control of one's person. Guardianship wars.

As you already know from reading earlier parts of this book, that legal fight is not limited to will contests, and trust lawsuits <u>after</u> one dies. The guardianship court is the new venue for the probate wars when someone is slipping, or failing mentally. Keep this in mind as you plan your estate. It may just force you to consider whether your adult children will make trouble for your latest spouse if you become incompetent. It may also make you consider: who do you love more? ….your adult children who don't visit…..or your latest spouse?

Finally, consider this in light of who you choose to be your successor trustee of your revocable trust, your attorney-in-fact under your durable power of attorney, and who you want to make health care decisions for you.

As we discussed in the first part of this chapter, if you lose capacity, that may mean that your latest spouse has to ask your successor trustee for money to live on. If that successor trustee is an adult child from a prior relationship who does not get along with your latest spouse, this can create guardianship wars. Or at least prolong them.

'Nough said.

3. **<u>Your kids will sue you.</u>**

Yes, your children will sue you. They may sue you as trustee of your own revocable trust seeking a determination from a court that you are not competent to serve as your own trustee.

Or, your adult children may be the ones filing a guardianship action. They may want to control you and your money. And, perhaps your latest spouse, too.

This may come as a shock or a surprise. But just imagine that you are in your living room one day, and a knock at the door is not Fed Ex or UPS. It's a process server who "serves" with "guardianship papers" informing you that your adult children from your first marriage are asking a court to control you and your money. And they didn't even tell you in advance.

4. **Your kids will tell you it's for your own good**.

A son or daughter suing a parent can be both shocking, and confusing, to the parent.

Well, that's what happens when an adult child "files" a guardianship petition, or "opens up" a guardianship matter, or "files for guardianship."

Many times, there are very good reasons to do this.

But, as you can guess, there are guardianship wars out there. Guardianship filings which are not motivated by good reasons. In actuality, many times your adult son or daughter will file for guardianship because they want to control you or your property. They don't like your new boyfriend or girlfriend or partner. They are worried about losing their inheritance.

And they will tell you that suing you and filing for guardianship was for your own good.

Are your estate plan and your estate planning attorney ready for this?

5. **They changed your estate plan!**

What?
They changed your estate plan!
What?
One thing that you should talk to your estate planning lawyer about is to what extent a guardianship court will permit your existing estate plan to change.

Some guardianship laws permit, under certain circumstances, usually only with court approval or supervision, a change to your existing estate plan, if you are found to be incapacitated or not competent.

In my book, **Pankauski's Probate Litigation Guide**, Chapter 10 deals with how they change your estate plan **after** you die through the legal concepts of *modification* and *reformation* of wills and trusts.

Yes, after you pass away, even if you think your will or trust is *ir*revocable, the dirty truth is that it can be changed, or modified, or reformed. This is <u>startling to most people</u> who think that they have an ironclad estate plan or a trust which can never be altered.

The same thing may be possible if you lose capacity and if there is a guardianship.

Most state guardianship laws have some sort of mechanism to also give away your property, for example, if it is in accordance with your ongoing intent, or "gifting" history. The most common example might be if you are making annual, ongoing gifts of, say, $14,000, to children and grandchildren. Another common example is the paying of college tuition for family members. Yet another is the mom or dad who "help out" an adult child with regular gifts of money or living expenses, support, or a mortgage or car payment. If you have the money, and intent, to make such family gifts—the argument goes – why not have the guardianship continue them as long as you have adequate money for your own care?

However, there *is* the opportunity for abuse of the guardianship process. For example, we could all imagine the "bad" guardian making distributions of money from the guardianship account, without court approval, of gifts to the guardian and all her or his children and spouses. Such self-dealing is not permitted. Guardians need to account for every last dime—or, rather, they are supposed to.

Likewise, your existing estate plan—what your will or trust says —can be altered or changed improperly. Consider this scenario.

You are a wealthy widowed woman who has a falling out with one of your two adult children—your only son. You do what a number of people do across the country every week: you decide to radically change your estate plan. You have your estate planning attorney change your last will and also your revocable trust with a codicil and trust amendment disinheriting your son.

Now, after you sign the codicil to your will, and your trust amendment, your estate plan "says" that your only daughter inherits everything. You also remove your son as your named successor co-trustee of your trust, and now have your daughter as your only successor trustee.

Bad son "out." Good daughter "in." That is, until…….

Somehow, your son learns of this trust amendment. Upon learning of his dis-inheritance, your son hires an elder law attorney and runs to the guardianship court and convinces a probate court judge that you don't have at least some of your capacity. The court appoints your son as your Emergency Temporary Guardian, who then files a motion with the guardianship court to have the codicil to your will, and your latest amendment to the trust "voided." Your son claims that you executed the codicil and trust amendment, which removed him as a beneficiary and as a co-trustee, at a time when you lacked the requisite mental capacity.

Could this happen? Yes.

Does this happen? Yes. This is an example of an abuse of the guardianship process by a greedy disinherited son.

Do you, and your estate planning attorney, know how to protect against such mis-use of the guardianship process?

CHAPTER 7

your limited capacity, guardianship estate plan

3 documents you definitely need

There are three documents which you should consider having as part of your estate plan, in addition to a will: a revocable trust, a power of attorney, and health care documents.

If you have these documents, you will have your "team" in place should you not be able to make decisions, pay your bills, or manage your money.

I know that most people think of an estate plan, or at least a *simple* estate plan, as a Last Will, and jointly-owned assets with the right of survivorship. And, indeed, sometimes simple is better.

But you should at least consider planning for your incapacity with a little more fire power.

Consider: Who is going to handle your affairs if you can't? Who will determine where you reside, and who you reside with? Who do you want determining your level of health care, and who provides medical services, and where you should receive those services? Who will be in charge of all your money? Who do you trust to manage your property and protect it?

Why not consider making those choices now, and putting it all down in writing?

A **revocable trust,** or **living trust,** can be thought of as your property management system. You can change or amend this at any time that you are competent. You cannot alter, amend or restate your revocable trust if you are not competent.

What is "competent?"

Generally, we think of being "not competent", or incapable of signing, or executing, a will or trust as not being able to understand the implications of what you are doing. Said another way: do you understand the nature and extent of your property? Who inherits under your then existing will or trust? Do you understand who your existing relatives and beneficiaries are? Do you understand who you are "cutting out," or not leaving an inheritance to, or how you are changing your estate plan, when you sign will or trust, or make a change?

Probate litigators refer to one who is incompetent *as not possessing the requisite mental capacity* to execute the will or trust.

On the other side of that legal coin, what does it mean when a person is competent to change or alter an estate plan, or to sign a will or trust?

The legal bar or threshold may not be particularly high in some instances. Some courts have held that it is not necessary to be super-sharp, to know each and every element of your then existing estate plan, nor to be able to recite an exhaustive list of all your assets and properties. No, if you, at the moment when you sign a will or trust, have a *general understanding* of what you are doing, you may, indeed, be competent.

What does a revocable trust look like?

A typical revocable trust's terms will instruct the trustee to distribute money to you and for your benefit during life, without any money going to anyone else (other than to pay your bills, or, maybe, your spouse). It's exclusively yours during your life. (Many times, for long term marriages, many trust creators, or "settlors", will also instruct the trustee to distribute money to one's spouse.)

In your trust, you can choose who you want to manage your money when you are not there. So, after your death, do you want to just distribute your trust money outright, without a trust, as an inheritance to your chosen beneficiaries? If so, that's fine and easy to do. But, if you want to retain some "control from the grave", and keep money in trust, and keep a trust fund, for, say, your surviving spouse or grand-children, consider who should be your successor trustees.

Just realize that your successor trustees, who you name to take control of the trust in your trust document, don't just serve when you die. Your successor trustees also serve as trustee when you are unable to serve. Such as if, for example, you become incapacitated.

So, give careful thought to who you want to "run your money", and administer your wealth, when you can't. If you read my first book, ***Pankauski's Trustee's Guide: 10 Steps to Family Trustee Excellence***, you know that I believe serving as a trustee is, generally, best left to the pro's. And by professionals, I mean banks and trust companies, certainly not trust lawyers.

> *Can a person in a guardianship matter be divorced?*

Now, most closely-married, or long term, couples permit the trustee to make distributions to your spouse during your life, but this is not always the case, such as in second or third marriages. Note, however, that you generally can't keep assets in a trust and keep that money away from your creditors, or your spouse. Sort of.

Most states recognize that each spouse has an obligation to support the other spouse *during marriage.* Translation? If you are incapacitated or incompetent and you are married, your trustee is going to use your trust funds for the support and maintenance of you, your lifestyle and your spouse's.

Needless to say, interesting issues arise when someone files for divorce and one party is not competent. Or, vice versa: a guardianship is filed, and then a spouse, or the alleged incapacitated person's adult children, want a divorce for the alleged incapacitated person.

Sometimes, there are restrictions on when an incompetent person, or one's guardian, may, or may not, seek, or be granted, a divorce. As you can image, with so many second and third marriages out there, divorce becomes a very important issue when one spouse becomes incapacitated.

Finally, please note that we have been discussing your <u>revocable</u> trust, which you create. We are not discussing trusts which were, from the beginning, ***ir***revocable, or created by others for your benefit. These so called irrevocable trusts operate by different rules.

A **power of attorney** document is a *fiduciary* relationship where you grant, or give to, someone the authority to act for you. It is sometimes referred to as an agency, even though the person you give the authority to (called the *power holder*, your *agent*, or *attorney in fact*) has an obligation to work for you and to act in your best interests. As such, an attorney in fact should not engage in acts of self-dealing, conflicts of interest, or civil theft or larceny.

The ***attorney in fact*** can pay your bills, file your income taxes, make sure your real estate taxes and health care providers (e.g. nurses aids or caretakers) are paid. I know what you are thinking: my spouse will handle all of that. That's fine, but what if your spouse is not around or not able to handle all your bills or manage your money? What if your spouse becomes incapacitated a few years after you do? Who is in charge then? Always consider having back up or successor fiduciaries.

You should know the limits of your power of attorney, and consider cutting edge legal issues which can arise.

Can a power of attorney amend your trust, or "order" your trustee around? Can your attorney in fact make gifts to himself or herself, or change the beneficiary designations on your IRA, life insurance policies and bank accounts? Can a power of attorney file for divorce from your spouse?

You should have an in depth discussion with your estate planning attorney on the limitations and risks of giving someone such authority.

Never, ever, create a POA with someone you don't trust.

Regrettably, in Florida, the lawyers in our firm witness cases where people mis-use a power of attorney to improperly take property or change bank accounts or beneficiaries.

Finally, your estate plan should contain health care and guardianship documents, which give someone close to you authority to make decisions regarding your medical treatment if you can't make such decisions. As discussed in Chapter 5, states have different names for these documents. Just know what you want, and whether the documents give you what you want.

One final word on these important estate planning documents. They force you to pick favorites…… to name a trustee, or a health care decision maker, or POA. That causes anxiety for some people, because a spouse, or a child, or loved one, may feel jealous or hurt if they are not selected.

And, in my opinion, selecting everyone, or all your children, is not the way to go. I don't advise having a number of people as your "power of attorney", or having multiple co-trustees. Running your life by committee can cause other issues. My advice: be selfish and focus on you, yourself, and your care and estate plan — and not others' feelings. Try to select one individual, who you trust, to serve as your decision maker.

It's your life and your money. Install into positions of fiduciary leadership those that you think will do the best job, and help you the most, regardless that someone's feelings may be hurt. If they love you, they should respect your decisions.

And always, always, be leery of someone who is pushing you repeatedly to *"put them on"* the power of attorney, or someone who insists on being your trustee.

Talk to your estate planning attorney about the best way to approach this. If you end up in probate litigation, your lawyer's testimony, and his or her notes, can be your best bet to uphold the estate plan which *you* want.

CHAPTER 8

the money chase

*elder abuse, financial exploitation
& monetary predators*

Sadly, Florida has more than it's "fair" share of financial exploitation.

Financial abuse directed to the elderly is so widespread, that many sheriffs' offices, and state attorneys' offices, have special units dedicated to financial exploitation of our senior citizens.

What is important to know is that monetary or financial predators are out there. And they may not be who you believe them to be.

They don't look like hoodlums or thugs, or have a sign on their chest with a brazen warning. They don't dress like Al Capone. A quick Google or Yahoo search will reveal stories which demonstrate that they may be your neighbors, caretakers, "friends" and even those in a fiduciary position.

Many times, they are your adult children or in-laws.

Financial exploitation doesn't necessary involve force or violence. It can involve increased pressure, so called "undue influence", over-persuasion, over-reaching, and veiled threats.

Financial exploitation can start off innocent enough. Friends, neighbors or family members ask, or offer, to assist with your banking needs, paying your bills, or helping with business decisions.

Abuse of trust, or a fiduciary position, are common, recurring themes in the world of financial exploitation.

People mis-use a power of attorney to "deed" your property to themselves. They mis-use access to your financial accounts by changing beneficiaries, or beneficiary designations, on things like insurance contracts, annuities, brokerage accounts, and mutual funds – and name themselves (the exploiter) as the "joint owner" or new beneficiary.

Bad trustees or co-trustees of your revocable trust can mis-use your ATM card, or credit cards, to withdraw money, or incur costs and expenses that are not for your benefit, but for their own use.

How can you begin to guard against financial exploitation, which may or may not occur in the future, when you may (or may not) be "slipping" or declining?

Having a trusted CPA, banker or trust officer, and estate planning attorney, can be one way to protect you. The good, trusted family advisers that I know and admire indeed love helping their clients, enjoy their work, and sincerely place their clients' interests above everyone else's, including their own. Good service providers are hard to find, and God knows that they can be pricey. But the alternative –not to have anyone in your corner – is not comforting.

What do these advisers suggest? What are some of their pointers and best pieces of advise?

<u>Avoid</u> the get rich quick scams and the incredible investment returns that promoters tease you with.

<u>Walk away</u> from the "new kid in town" who's selling investment services or the "next big thing" that no one seems to know about.

<u>Say "no"</u> to investment schemes that you don't understand.

<u>Run from</u> someone "forcing you" to sign, or repeatedly asking you for, a POA.

<u>Watch out</u> for someone who always asks you to become your trustee or to be "put on" your bank accounts.

<u>Consider</u> banks and trust departments that invest in things that you can get your arms around, like bonds and marketable securities. And good cold cash. Your banker, trustee or successor trustee, should know your estate plan, CPA, know who your estate attorney is, and "who gets what" when you are gone.

The trial lawyers in our firm can tell you tales of family members that would make you cringe. Sisters, brothers, daughters and sons, using mom or dad's checking account and credit cards for personal expenses, travel, airport lunches, and grocery store purchases.

Second and third spouses, or adult step-children, transferring mom or dad's, or your spouse's money, in the name of "safeguarding" it and securing it.

Deeds get signed and real estate "goes" into someone else's name. Financial accounts get "inherited" by the exploiter who got their name placed on the account as a "pay on death" beneficiary.

What's most important is that you recognize that you can lose your property and money as you age and get more vulnerable. And it's not always limited to Ponzi-schemes or Madoff-like scams.

So, discuss with your estate planning attorney what steps you can take, now, to set up a system, or team, to safeguard your property with the correct legal documents and with trusted, reliable fiduciaries and advisors.

CONCLUSION

Guardianships for adults are on the rise.

And so are hotly contested guardianship lawsuits among family members, in-laws, outlaws, 2nd and 3rd spouses, and adult children from a marriage or relationship years ago.

When we decline, or start to lose it, family members often vie for control. They hire litigators to fight in guardianship court about who will make decisions for us, and who will handle our money and property. Even across the miles and over the years. Even if a family member has been estranged or not involved in your life for years.

If your latest spouse doesn't get along with your adult children from your first marriage now, imagine how they will act if you are not around. Imagine how they will deal with each other if you are incapacitated. Or, if you are in such mental decline, that you are there <u>physically</u>, but not mentally.

As we age, our bodies can keep going but our mental faculties can decline, making things which were once easy seem challenging.

Our ability to handle the most simple tasks related to our property, or personal choices, diminishes. We become more susceptible to others. Including family members. Including those who may be motivated by a desire to get your money, or control your property.

Yes, we become potential victims of undue influence, financial exploitation and elder abuse.

Many times, these wrongs are not just committed by strangers or thugs, but, rather, by family members and fiduciaries.

Knowing that those around you, now, or in the future, may, or may not, fight over you, your control and your property, may be eye-opening.

Who will make decisions for you and your property is serious business.

And guardianship courts, or probate courts, hear these matters every day in the USA. Guardianship filings involve, after all, your human rights, and your freedoms and civil liberties.

And whether or not you have your rights and liberties taken away.

And, if so, who will exercise your rights, or control you and your property. Who will make decisions for you?

Use the lessons and observations learned in ***Pankauski's Guardianship Wars*** to work with your estate planning lawyer, now, to prepare for incapacity. Choosing your fiduciaries carefully, now, can be an important step to eliminating or minimizing future guardianship litigation.

INDEX

A

active seniors, 9–11
adult children
    financial control and, 76–78
    as "interested persons", 28
    lawsuits by, 77
    and parental prenups, 71–72
    sibling rivalries, 8
    vs. spouses, 75–76
    see also family members
alleged incapacitated person (AIP)
    court-appointed counsel for, 44–46
    determining mental health of, 42
    filing a guardianship against, 32–33
    testimony by, 46
asset transfer, 61
attorney in fact. *see* power of attorney

attorneys
    for alleged incapacitated persons, 44–46
    elder law, 3, 37, 47
    incapacity planning with, 52
    for individual family members, 45
    payments to estate, 25
    testimony by estate-planning, 94
    with trial skills, 46–47

B

beneficiaries, changing, 98

C

caregiving
    determining adequacy of, 56
    planning for, 53–55
Chapter 744, Florida Statutes, 36

children, adult. *see* adult children
civil liberties
    broad guardianships curb, 18, 34
    judges' respect for, 41
    POA as administering, 63–64
civil theft, 65
competence
    estate planning and, 49–51
    to execute trusts, 86–88
    guardianship court determines, 6, 19, 32–33
    see also incapacity
complaint, filing a, 39
control
    guardianship as, 21, 29, 77, 103
    of person and property, 34, 47
    by power of attorney, 65
    predetermining, 54–55
costs
    of guardianship, 57
    of probate litigation, 25

D

dementia, 13–14
disinheritance, 81–82
divorce, 90–91
"do not resuscitate" orders, 67
durable power of attorney
    for healthcare decisions, 64
    medical, 66
    in plan for incapacity, 62–63

E

elder law lawyers
    guardianship litigation by, 37
    hiring, 3
    with trial skills, 47
emergency temporary guardian
    asset transfer by, 62
    court-appointed, 40
    to manage affairs, 34
estate planning
    annual review of, 67
    arguments against, 56
    to avoid guardianships, 49–51
    to avoid probate, 24
    competence to change, 86–88
    difficult decisions in, 93–94
    documents needed for, 85
    for durable power of attorney, 62
    and family "favorites", 93–94
    as financial abuse protection, 102
    guardianship changes to, 79–82
    incapacity plans in, 52–54
    legal help for, 3, 98
    as lesser restrictive alternative, 59
    need for thorough, 104–105
    power of attorney in. *see* power of attorney
    prenups for, 72
    trustee familiarity with, 100
examining committee
    court-appointed, 40

work done by, 42, 43
    written reports by, 43–44
exploitation, financial, 96–97

F

family law court, 36
family members
    "backstory" of, 34
    control by, 103
    and emotional trust, 93–94
    vs. estate plan, 56
    feuds between, 76, 103–104
    financial abuse by, 97, 100
    financial gifts to, 80
    guardianships and conflict among, 43
    as "interested persons", 26, 28, 46
    lawyers for individual, 45
    as power of attorneys, 64–65
fiduciary. *see* power of attorney
filing guardianships
    actions resulting from, 40
    by adult children, 77, 78
    as allegation of incapacity, 39–40
    estate planning to avoid, 50, 54
    by "interested persons", 27–29
financial abuse, 96, 104
Florida, 11
Florida Statues Chapter 744, 36

G

gifting history, 80
grantor of living trusts, 60
guardian ad litem, 35

guardians
    court-determined, 40
    divorce proceedings by, 90–91
    emergency temporary, 34, 40, 62
    as managers of affairs, 33–34
    for minors, 35
    of person and property, 47, 61
    predetermining, 67
    rights as controlled by, 33
    self-dealing by "bad", 81
    trial to determine, 46
    trusts as replacing, 63
Guardianship Code, 36
guardianship court
    conveying intent to, 51–52
    defined, 36
    filing petitions with, 39–40
    judges, 40–42, 47
    mental health determinations by, 40–42
    predetermination as recognized by, 54–55
guardianship litigation
    for control, 21–22, 23–24
    before death, 18, 23
    eliminating future, 105
    vs. estate plan, 55
    examining committee reports in, 44
    example of, 8
    by feuding family members, 75
    and impatience of children, 15–16
    increase in, 6, 7, 37

post-WWII prevalence of,
  14–15
as probate war
  battlefield, 19
reasons for, 9–16
guardianships
  alternatives to, 33, 49–57
  avoiding, 49–51, 57
  cost of, 57
  discovering "backstory" of,
    34–35
  filing. *see* filing
    guardianships
  increase in, 103
  "interested persons" in,
    26–28
  invasiveness of, 42
  laws governing, 36
  mis-use of, 79–82
  partial or plenary, 33, 44
  of person and property, 34
  petitioners in, 32
  and prenups, 70–75
  as probate war battlefield,
    31–32
  for protection vs control, 29
  removal of rights by, 32
  as trials, 46

H

healthcare
  advances in, 12–14
  decisions by power of
    attorney, 64
  documents, 66
  proxy, 66
hearing, guardianship, 46
impatience, 15–16
incapacity
  and conveying intent, 51–52

court-determined, 32,
  40–42
determining mental, 29, 87
and divorce, 90–91
and durable power of
  attorney, 62–63
and estate plan changes, 80
filing allegations of, 39–40
guardian to assist with, 22,
  33–34
"interested persons" and,
  26, 28, 82
likelihood of, 12
medical decisions
  during, 93
planning for, 2, 49–51, 86
and prenup changes, 73–74
preparations for, 103–
  104, 105
selecting care team for,
  53–54
and successor trustees, 60,
  88–89
inheritance
  by beneficiaries, 100
  and disinheritance, 81–82
  family feuds over, 78
  impatience over, 15–16
  posthumous fights over, 17
  vs. trusts, 88–89
interested persons, 26–28, 46
investment advice, 98–99
irrevocable trusts, 91

L

Last Will, 85
lawyers. *see* attorneys
legal actors, 26
life support, 66, 67
litigation

by adult children, 77
guardianship. *see*
    guardianship
    litigation
probate. *see* probate
    litigation
to resolve family
    disputes, 23
trust, 15, 35–36
living trust. *see* trust, living
living will, 66
longevity and mental decline, 7, 9

M

marriage
    divorce and incapacity, 90–91
    spousal support during, 89–90
    "take nothing" prenup, 70–75
medical decisions, 64, 66, 93, 105
medical power of attorney, 66
mental capacity. *see*
    competence
mental decline
    drugs to slow, 13–14
    and execution of trusts, 87
    guardianships for those in, 31
    longevity and, 7
    and prenup changes, 73–74
    and prevention of financial abuse, 98
    rate of progressive, 11–12
    vulnerability of, 104
mental health
    court-determined, 40–42
    examining committee expertise in, 43
    see also competence
minors, guardians for, 35
money
    financial abuse, 96–101
    financial power of attorney, 60
    gifting history, 80
    guardianship as control over, 29, 47
    and prenups, 71–72
    trustees as managing, 60–61, 89–90

P

Pankauski's Guardianship Wars, 26
Pankauski's Probate Litigation Guide: Top 10 Probate Mistakes Revealed, 14, 25, 65, 75
Pankauski's Trustee's Guide: 10 Steps to Family Trustee Excellence, 14, 89
partial guardianships, 33, 44
persistent vegetative state, 66
person, guardian of your, 47, 61
petition, filing a, 39
petitioner, guardianship, 32
plenary guardianships, 33, 44
power of attorney
    asset transfer by, 61
    backups to, 91–92
    durable, 62–63
    limits of, 92
    mis-use of, 65, 92–93, 97–98
    one person as, 64–65, 93–94

for property management,
    60, 105
pushy would-be, 94, 99
responsibilities of, 91–92
prenups, 70–75
probate court, 26
probate litigation
    and attorney testimony, 94
    cost of, 25
    guardianships and, 23,
        31, 37
    modern prevalence of, 15
    for objections to estate
        plan, 24–25
    and power of attorney
        misuse, 65

R

revocable trusts. *see* trust,
    living
rights, human and legal
    broad guardianships
        curb, 34
    examining committee's
        report on, 44
    power of attorney as
        administering, 63–64
    removed based on
        incapacity, 32

S

seniors
    financial abuse of, 96
    healthy, active, 9–11
settlor of living trusts, 60
sibling rivalries, 8
simple guardianships, 6, 19
spouses
    vs. adult children, 75–76
    financial abuse by, 100

as "interested persons", 28
named in estate plans, 68
and prenups, 70–75
vs. stepchildren, 8, 16–17
trusts as supporting, 89–90
stepchildren, 16–17
successor trustees
    choosing, 60, 63
    vs. other family
        members, 76
    posthumous funding of,
        88–89

T

"take nothing" prenup, 70–75
temporary guardians, 34, 40
trial, guardianship, 46
trust, irrevocable, 79–80
trust, living
    annual review of, 67–68
    asset transfer into, 61–62
    competence to execute,
        87–88
    components of, 88
    vs. irrevocable, 91
    power of attorney
        amendments to, 92
    for property management,
        63, 86
    trustees for, 60
trust litigation
    guardians for minors in,
        35–36
    modern prevalence of, 15
trustees
    choosing, 60
    financial abuse by, 98
    professional, 89
    pushy would-be, 94, 99

W

West Palm Beach, Florida, 9
wills
    estate planning to enhance, 59
    living, 66
    objections to, 24
    posthumous changes to, 79–80

ABOUT THE AUTHOR

John Pankauski leads a boutique litigation and appellate firm in West Palm Beach, which handles trials and appeals of family & business disputes throughout Florida. Through his trials and appeals, he has seen billions of dollars move back and forth between trusts, estates, widows, ne'er do wells, 2nd and 3rd spouses and the lawyers! He now shares his battle-drawn experiences with senior family members (who made the money), executors, dis-inherited heirs, and beneficiaries. Also by John Pankauski: Pankauski's Trustee's Guide: 10 Steps to Family Trustee Excellence and Pankauski's Probate Litigation Guide: Top 10 Probate Mistakes Revealed.

www.ingramcontent.com/pod-product-compliance
Lightning Source LLC
Chambersburg PA
CBHW021545200526
45163CB00015B/1662